Brick

LEARNING
COUNTING AND
CARDINALITY
USING
LEGO® BRICKS
STUDENT EDITION

Dr. Shirley Disseler

COMPASS

Learning Counting and Cardinality Using LEGO® Bricks — Student Edition

Brigantine Media/Compass Publishing
211 North Avenue
St. Johnsbury, Vermont 05819
Phone: 802-751-8802
Fax: 802-751-8804
E-mail: neil@brigantinemedia.com
Website: www.compasspublishing.org

ORDERING INFORMATION

Quantity sales
Special discounts for schools are available for quantity purchases of physical books and digital downloads. For information, contact Brigantine Media at the address shown above or visit www.compasspublishing.org.

Individual sales
Brigantine Media/Compass Publishing publications are available through most booksellers. They can also be ordered directly from the publisher.
Phone: 802-751-8802 | Fax: 802-751-8804
www.compasspublishing.org
ISBN 978-1-9384066-4-5

CONTENTS

PATTERNS

Part 1

1. Build a color pattern model with two different colors of 1x1 bricks. Continue the color pattern three times. Draw your model and describe the pattern.

2. Build a **size pattern** model with three different sizes of bricks. Continue the **size pattern** two times. Draw your model and describe the pattern.

3. Build a **number pattern** model with four numbers. Continue the **number pattern** two times. Draw your model and describe the pattern.

_____

_____

_____

_____

_____

_____

_____

4. Build a model that is both a **number and color pattern** with three terms. Continue the pattern two times. Draw your model and describe the pattern.

_____

_____

_____

_____

_____

_____

_____

Part 2

1. Can you build a pattern model that has four colors? Draw your model and describe the pattern.

_____

_____

_____

_____

_____

_____

_____

2. Can you build a pattern model that has at least three sizes of bricks? Draw your model and describe the pattern.

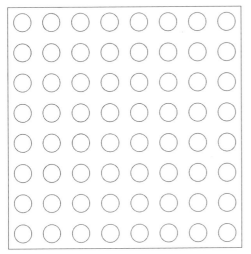

_____

_____

_____

_____

_____

_____

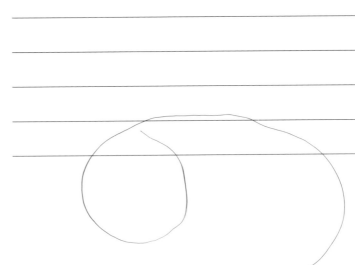

3. Can you build a number pattern model that shows 2, 4, 6, 2, 4, 6? Draw your model and describe the pattern.

_____

_____

_____

_____

_____

_____

4. Can you design and build a pattern model that is both a color pattern and a number pattern? Draw your model and describe the pattern.

_____

_____

_____

_____

_____

_____

Challenge:

Design and build a pattern model. Find a partner. Exchange pattern models. Draw your partner's model and describe the pattern.

Partner's model:

_____

_____

_____

_____

_____

_____

_____

Assessment

1. What does it mean to make a pattern?

_____

_____

2. Build a color pattern model. Draw your model and describe the pattern.

_____

_____

_____

_____

_____

_____

_____

3. Build a number pattern model. Draw your model and describe the pattern.

_____

_____

_____

_____

_____

4. Build a model that has two types of patterns in it. Draw your model and describe the patterns.

_____

_____

_____

_____

_____

_____

WHAT IS A NUMBER?

Part 1

1. Build a model that shows 1 single stud. Draw your model and describe it.

_____

_____

_____

_____

_____

_____

2. Using another color of bricks, build a model that shows 2 single studs. Draw your model and describe it.

_____

_____

_____

_____

_____

_____

3. Using a third color of bricks, build a model that shows 3 single studs. Draw your model and describe it.

_____

_____

_____

_____

_____

_____

_____

4. Place all three models side by side. Build a model that would be the next step in the pattern.

This model has _____ studs.

This model has   _more_   or   _less_   (circle one) studs than the model in problem 3.

Part 2

1. Can you build a model that shows five studs? Use bricks that are all the same color. Draw your model. Describe your model and label each number.

_____

_____

_____

_____

_____

_____

_____

2. Can you build a model that shows six studs? Use bricks that are all the same color. Draw your model. Describe your model and label each number.

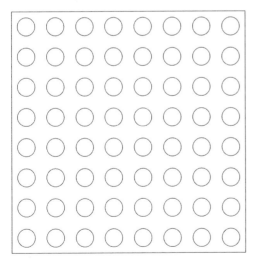

_____

_____

_____

_____

_____

_____

_____

3. Can you build a model that has three more studs than the model you built for problem 1 (Part 2)? Draw your model and describe it.

More Problems to Practice:

4. Build two different models that show the same amount.

Model 1

Model 2

How many studs are in Model 1?
_____studs

How many studs are in Model 2?
_____studs

5. Build two models. The second model should have 2 studs less than the first model.

Model 1

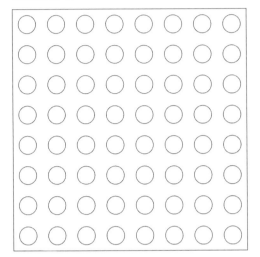

How many studs are in Model 1?
_____studs

Model 2

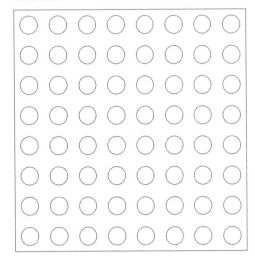

How many studs are in Model 2?
_____studs

Assessment

1. How many studs are in this model? _____ studs

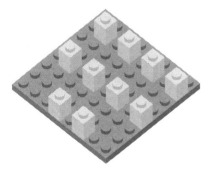

2. Build a model that shows six studs. Draw and describe your model.

_____

_____

_____

_____

_____

_____

3. Make two models that show two different numbers. What numbers do the models show?

Model 1_____   Model 2_____

Which model has more?   Model 1   Model 2 (circle one). Draw both models.

Model 1

Model 2

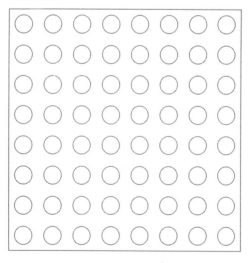

TEN-FRAMES

Part 1

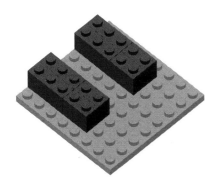

1. Build two ten-frames with bricks.

Count the studs. How many studs are in each ten-frame? _____

2. On one of the ten-frames, place 1x1 bricks on top of each stud.
Draw this ten-frame model.

3. On the second ten-frame, place enough 1x1 bricks to fill the top row of the ten-frame. Add the second ten-frame to the drawing and draw your model.

How many 1x1 bricks fit on the first ten-frame? _____

How many 1x1 bricks are on the top row of the second ten-frame? _____

How many 1x1 bricks are there in all? _____

4. Build a model that shows the number 12 using two ten-frames. Draw your model.

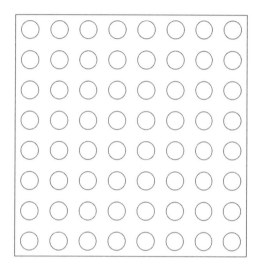

How many 1x1 bricks are on the first ten-frame? _____

How many 1x1 bricks are on the second ten-frame? _____

How many studs are there in all? _____

5. Build a new model using one or two ten-frames. Do not show it to your partner until both have been completed. After you have finished, share your models. Talk about which model has more and which one has less. Draw your model and your partner's model. Circle the one that has more.

My model

My partner's model

Part 2

1. Can you build the number 14 using two ten-frame models? Draw your model. Label the model to show tens and ones.

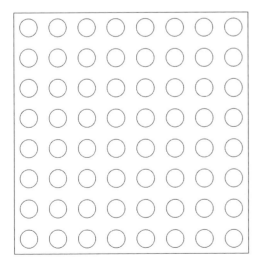

My model has _____ tens.

My model has _____ ones.

2. Using two ten-frames, build this model:

The first ten-frame should show three more than the second ten-frame. You must have at least two 1x1 bricks on the second ten-frame.

Draw your model.

The first ten-frame has _____ studs.

The second ten-frame has _____ studs.

The first ten-frame has (circle one) *more than* or *less than* the second ten-frame.

There are _____ studs in all.

My model shows the number _____.

3. Ten-Frame Game:

Build a model of any number up to 20 using no more than two ten frames.

Draw your model.

How many studs does this model have? _____studs

Find a partner who has a model that shows a number *more than* yours. How many studs does your partner's model have? _____

Find a partner who has a model that shows the *same* number as yours. How many studs does your partner's model have? _____

Find a partner who has a model that shows a number *less than* your model. How many studs does your partner's model have? _____

Challenge Problems:

4. Build four ten-frames. Can you model the number 24? Draw your model and label the tens and ones.

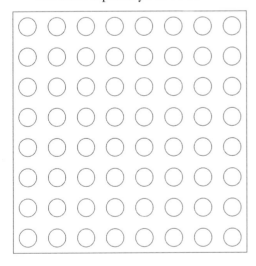

Explain your thinking:

My model has _____ studs.

My model has _____ sets of 10.

My model has _____ studs more than ten.

My model shows _____ studs in all.

5. Choose a number greater than 24. Can you model your number? Build and draw your model. Explain your model.

_____

_____

_____

Assessment

1. Build a model of one ten-frame. Place 1x1 bricks on the model to show the number 6. Draw your model.

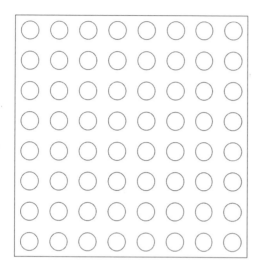

My ten-frame has _____ studs covered. The number

of studs not covered is _____.

2. Build two ten-frames. Use 1x1 bricks to show 1 ten and 3 ones. Label the tens and the ones. Draw your model.

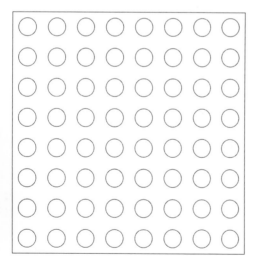

My model shows _____ 1x1 bricks on one ten-frame

and _____ 1x1 bricks on the other ten-frame.

Together my ten-frames show the number _____.

3. Model the number 26 using ten-frames and 1x1 bricks. Draw and label your model.

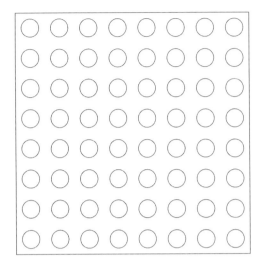

My model has _____ tens.

My model has _____ ones.

My model shows the number _____.

4. Which ten-frame model shows more? **A** or **B** (circle one)

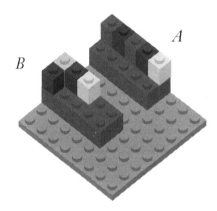

5. Which ten-frame model shows less? **A** or **B** (circle one)

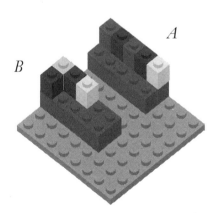

SKIP-COUNTING

Part 1

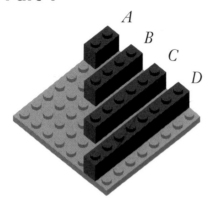

1. Build this model with bricks.

Record the number of studs in each column.

Column A: _____

Column B: _____

Column C: _____

Column D: _____

2. What do you notice about this model?

_____

_____

3. If you added to your model to continue the pattern, how many studs would the next group of bricks show? _____

4. Build a model that shows skip-counting by 3s. Begin with 3 and model the next three numbers. Draw your model.

5. Add the next number to your model. Draw it.

How many studs are in the next number? _____

Part 2

1. Can you build a model that shows skip-counting by 4s? Build at least three steps. Draw your model and label it to show how you counted.

2. Can you build a model that shows skip-counting by 5s? Build at least three steps. Draw your model and label it to show how you counted.

3. Can you build a model that shows skip-counting by 10s? Build at least three steps. Draw your model and label it to show how you counted.

4. Choose a number. Do not tell anyone your number. Can you model a skip-counting pattern with your secret number? Show your partner your model and have your partner identify the skip-count pattern. Draw your model and describe the pattern.

More Problems for Practice:

5. Build a model of a skip-count pattern that begins at 2. Skip-count by 3s. Model at least the first four numbers in the pattern. What is the fourth number in the pattern?
_____

Draw your model.

Assessment

1. Write the next three numbers if you begin to count at 3 and skip 3 each time.

3, _____, _____, _____

2. Build a model that shows a skip-counting pattern. Choose any number to start and skip-count three times. Draw your model.

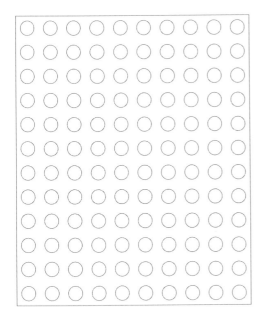

3. If you skip-count by 5s, how many times will you skip to get to 20? _____

JUMP NUMBERS

Part 1

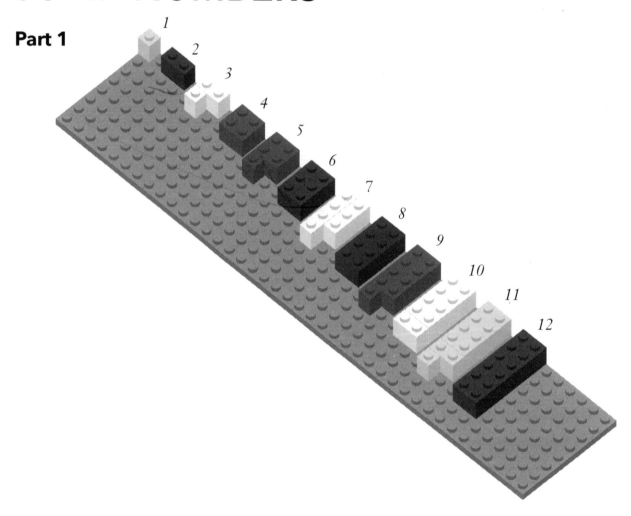

1. Look at the brick number line model. Build the same model with your bricks.

Draw your model and label each number.

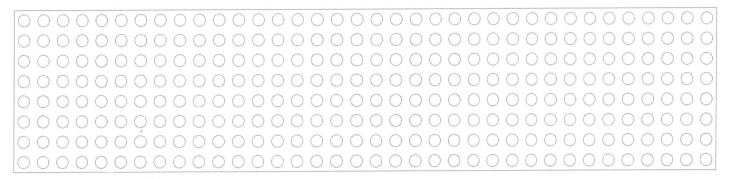

2. Build a model that shows counting by 2s. Start at 2 and show three more numbers in the pattern.

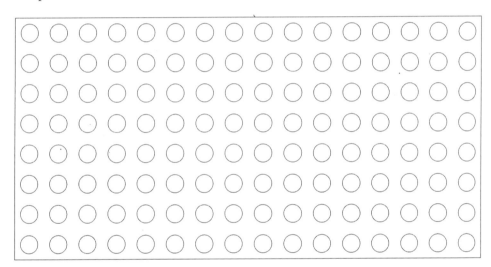

What number is next? _____ Add this to the model.
How do you know?

_____

_____

What is the pattern? _____, _____, _____, _____, _____

Draw your model and add the jump lines between each number.

How many equal jump lines can you draw between each number? _____

3. Build a model that shows counting by 4s. Build at least three numbers.

Draw your model and label each number. Label the jumps in the model.

How many jumps are there? _____

What is the pattern? _____, _____, _____, _____

What number comes next in the sequence? _____

How do you know?

_____

_____

_____

_____

4. Find a partner. One partner builds a model of even numbers. The other partner builds a model of odd numbers.

Draw your model and label the numbers.

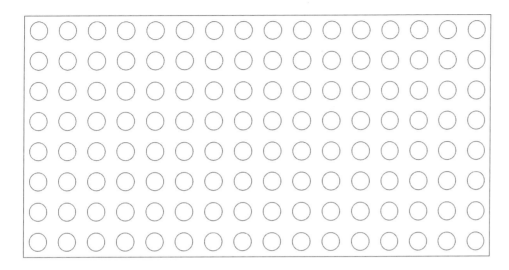

Look at your partner's model. How is that model different from your model?

_____

_____

Part 2

1. Build a brick number line that shows 1 to 10. Begin at the brick that represents the number 3. Counting by 2s, can you find the next three numbers in the sequence? Draw and label your model.

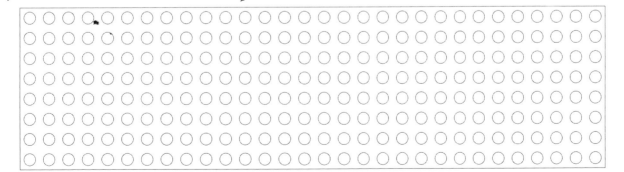

What are the next three numbers in the sequence? 3, _____, _____, _____

2. Build a brick number line that shows 1 to 12. Begin at the brick that represents the number 4. Counting by 3s, can you find the next two numbers in the sequence? Draw and label your model.

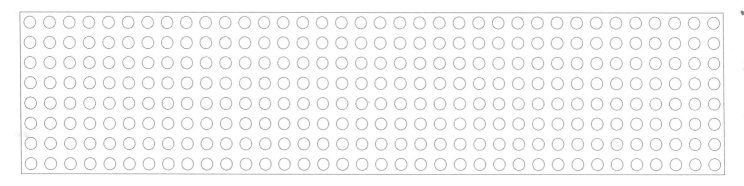

What are the next two numbers in the sequence? 4, _____, _____

3. Using the brick number line for 1 to 12, begin at the number 2. Can you find jumps of 2 until the end of the number line? How many jumps of 2 are there in the sequence? _____

Draw your model and label each jump of 2.

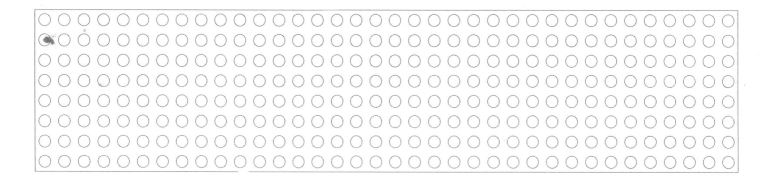

4. Can you build a model that shows both even and odd numbers? Draw your model. Circle all the even numbers in your model in red. Circle all the odd numbers in blue.

More Problems for Practice:

1. Make a model with 3 jumps in it. Draw your model.

What are the numbers in the model? _____

What is the pattern shown in the model? _____

Assessment

1. What is this number pattern? 3, 6, 9, 12, 15

Skip-counting by _____

Is the pattern odd or even? _____

(Build a model if you need to!)

2. Build a model that shows an odd number pattern with 3 to 5 terms. Do not begin with 1. Draw your model and label your solution.

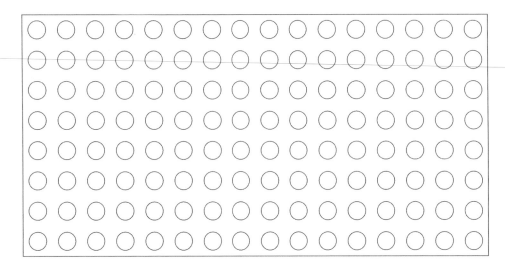

3. Build a model that shows an even number pattern with 3 to 5 terms. Do not begin with 2. Draw your model and label your solution.

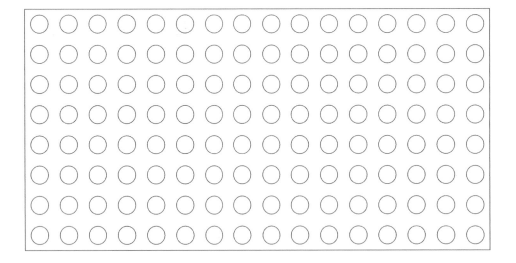

4. Build a 1 - 10 brick number line. Draw your model. Circle one even number and one odd number on the number line.

Using the model, how do you know a number is odd and a number is even?

_____

_____

Challenge Assessment
Draw a brick number line model of 1 – 12.

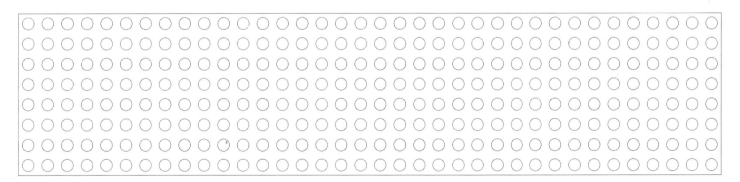

Use the number line to complete these tasks:

1. Label each number on the number line.

2. Beginning at the number 1, circle the jumps of 2 in red.

3. Beginning at the number 1, circle the jumps of 5 in blue.

4. If you begin at the number 6 and jump by 2s, how many jumps will it take to get to 12? _____

5. If you begin at the number 4 and jump three times by 4s, what number will you end on? _____

SQUARE NUMBERS

Part 1

1. Build the number 1 using a 1x1 brick. Draw your model.

2. Build the number two in 2 different ways using 2 different bricks. Draw your model.

3. Build the number three in 3 different ways using 3 different bricks. Draw your model.

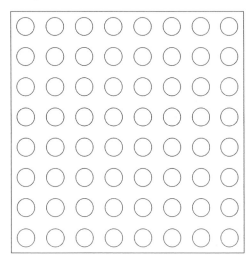

4. Build a model of the number 15 using fifteen 1x1 bricks with 5 across and 3 down. Draw your model.

What shape do you see when you look at the bricks in your model? _____

5. Rearrange the 1x1 bricks on your base plate to build another model of 15 that looks different than the last model of 15. Draw your model and describe it. How is the new model like the first one and how it is different?

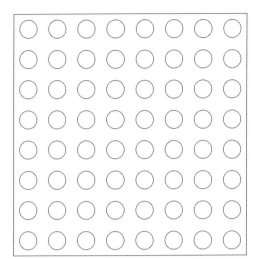

_____

_____

6. Build a model of the number 13 using 1x1 bricks. Describe how this model is different from the model of 15 that you built in number 5. Draw your model.

_____

_____

7. Build a model of two using one 1x2 brick. Draw your model.

Describe the shape of the model. _____

8. Place two 1x2 bricks side by side. Draw your model.

What shape is this model? _____

What number does it represent? _____

How is it different from the model that you built in number 7?

_____

_____

9. Build a model of 9 using three 1x3 bricks. Draw your model.

What shape is this model? _____

How does this model compare to the model that you built in number 8 ?

_____

_____

Part 2

1. Using 1x4 bricks, can you make a model showing 12 studs? Draw your model.

How many bricks did you use? _____

Write a description of your model. Is your model a square or a rectangle?

_____

_____

2. Using 1x1 bricks, can you build a model of the number 17? Draw your model. Compare your model with a partner. Draw your partner's model. Discuss how the models are alike and different. What do you notice about both your model and your partner's model? Write a description of your model.

My model

My partner's model

---

3. Can you build a model of another square number? Choose a number other than 4 or 9. Draw your model. Explain why it is a square number.

---

4. Choose a number greater than 10. Build a model of your number using bricks. Draw your model. What is your number? _____

Then:

• Find someone who has the same number model as you.

What is that number? _____

• Find someone who built a model that shows a number greater than yours.

What is that number? _____

• Find someone who built a model that shows a number less than yours.

What is that number? _____

More Problems for Practice:

5. Build a model of a square number and a model of rectangular number. Draw your models and describe your models. What number does each one represent?

_____

_____

_____

_____

_____

_____

6. Build a model of 16 that is square. Draw and explain your model.

_____

_____

_____

_____

_____

_____

Assessment

1. How are the numbers 9 and 6 different? Prove your answer by building a model. Explain your answer.

_____

_____

_____

_____

_____

2. Which of the following numbers is square? How do you know?

2   4   5   8

_____

_____

3. Make a model of a rectangular number. Draw your model. What number is it? Why is it rectangular?

_____

_____

_____

_____

_____

MORE THAN/LESS THAN

Part 1

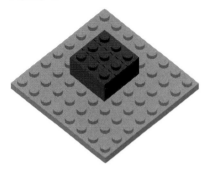

1. Build this model with bricks. How many studs are in the model? _____

Draw the model. Label this model *A*. Write a sentence that describes your model.

_____

_____

_____

_____

_____

2. Build a model that shows the number 10. Draw the model and label it *B*. Write a sentence that describes your model.

How many more studs does model B have than model A?_____

(grid of circles)

_____

_____

_____

_____

_____

_____

3. Build a model that has 12 studs.

Draw the model and Label it *C*. Write a sentence that describes your model.

(grid of circles)

_____

_____

_____

_____

_____

_____

Line up your models. Put the one with the least amount of studs first. Put the one with the most studs last. Write sentences that describe this order.

_____

_____

_____

_____

_____

4. Build a model that shows one less than the number of studs in model A. Draw the model and label it *D*. Write a sentence that describes these two models.

_____

_____

_____

5. Write the math symbol for *less than*. _____

Write the math symbol for *greater than*. _____

Write a math symbol that means the *same amount*. _____

6. Build the models shown.

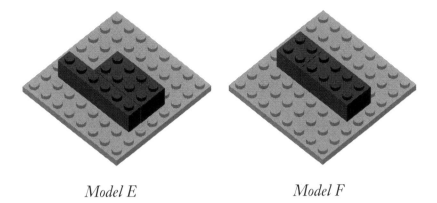

Model E   *Model F*

Write one *less than* statement about these models using math symbols. _____

Write one *greater than* statement about these models using math symbols. _____

Part 2

1. Build models of two numbers. Label your models A and B.

Can you write a *more than* statement about your model? Draw your models.

2. Build models of two numbers you did not use in problem 1. Label your models C and D.

Can you write a *less than* statement about your models? Draw your models.

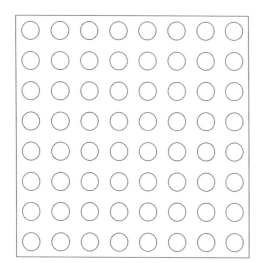

---

3. Build a comparison model using two different numbers. Draw your models.

Can you write two math statements using symbols for these models that show *less than* and *greater than*?

Challenge:

Build models of three different numbers. Draw your models.
Write as many math sentences as you can about these number models.

More Problems for Practice:

4. Build models of two numbers. One model should show 6 less than the other. Draw your models and write a math sentence about them.

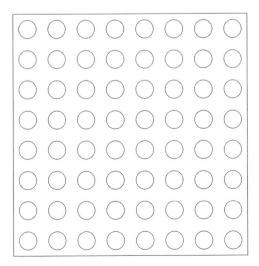

5. Build a model of any number. Show your partner your model. Write a *compare* statement about the two models. Draw both models.

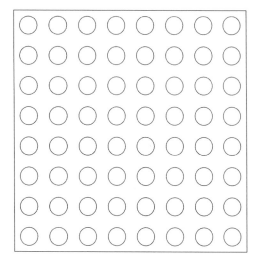

Assessment

1. Circle the math symbol for less than.   >   <   =

2. Circle the math symbol for greater than.   >   <   =

3. Circle the math symbol that means the same amount.   >   <   =

4. Build a model that shows two numbers. Write one *less than* math sentence and one *greater than* math sentence about your model. Draw your model.

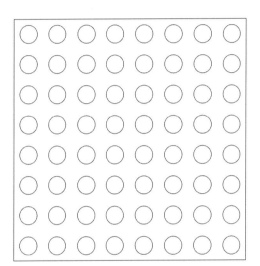

Greater than sentence: _____

Less than sentence: _____

COUNTING AND CARDINALITY
Student Assessment Chart

Name _____

Performance Skill	Not yet	With help	On target	Comments
I can count from 1 to 10.				
I can count objects by number.				
I can make a pattern using brick colors.				
I can make a pattern using studs to show numbers.				
I can skip-count by 2, 3, 5, and 10.				
I can count jumps between numbers on a number line.				
I can make a set of tens on a ten frame and count tens and ones.				
I can tell the name of a number in the tens place and in the ones place.				
I can identify numbers that are even and odd.				

Made in the USA
Columbia, SC
01 September 2018